D0200367

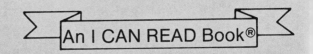

An I CAN READ Book®

Egg to Chick

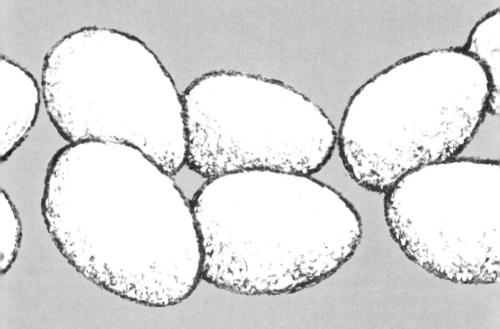

by Millicent E. Selsam
Pictures by Barbara Wolff

A Harper Trophy Book
HARPER & ROW, PUBLISHERS

I Can Read Book is a registered trademark of Harper & Row, Publishers, Inc.

EGG TO CHICK (Revised Edition)
Text copyright © 1946, 1970 by Harper & Row, Publishers, Inc.
Pictures copyright © 1970 by Barbara Wolff.
All rights reserved. Printed in the United States of America.
No part of this book may be used or reproduced
in any manner whatsoever without written permission
except in the case of brief quotations
embodied in critical articles and reviews.
For information address Harper & Row, Publishers, Inc.,
10 East 53rd Street, New York, N. Y. 10022.

Library of Congress Catalog Card Number: 74-85034.
ISBN 0-06-444113-X (pbk.)
First Harper Trophy edition, 1987

For Benjamin Wolff

Here is an egg.

How does an egg like this
grow into a
chicken like this?

Animals grow from eggs.

These eggs can become frogs.

These eggs can become turtles.

These eggs can become dogs.

These eggs can become chickens.

People grow from eggs too.

What makes an egg grow

into an animal?

An egg cannot grow

into an animal all by itself.

First, it must be joined by a sperm.

Then it will start growing

into a new animal.

The sperm comes from the father.

The egg comes from the mother.

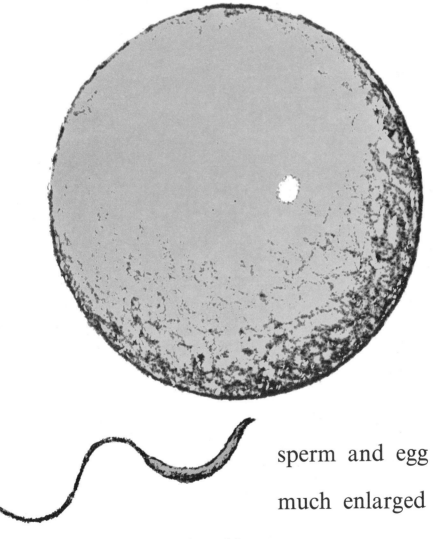

sperm and egg
much enlarged

That is why chickens and frogs

and dogs and people

all have both a mother and father.

The hen is the chick's mother.

The rooster is its father.

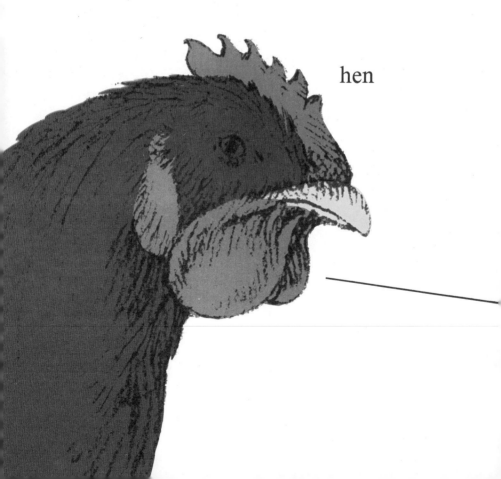

hen

rooster

chick

A hen's eggs begin to grow

inside her body.

Did you ever see the eggs

inside a chicken?

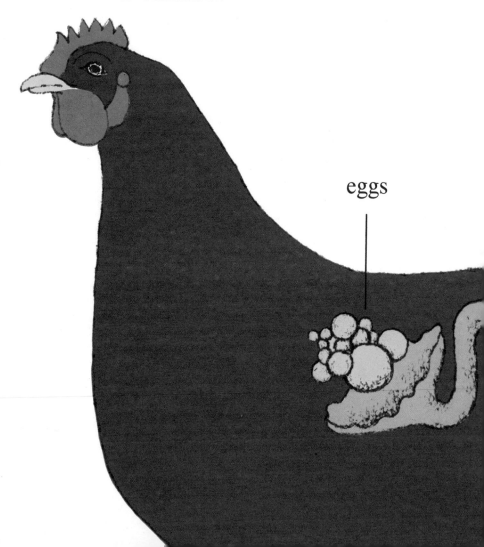

eggs

They are yellow because they are
full of yolk.

Soon they will go down the egg tube
in the hen.

The eggs are joined by sperm
before they enter the egg tube.

The rooster puts the sperm
into the egg tube in the hen's body.

Lots of sperm swim up the egg tube.

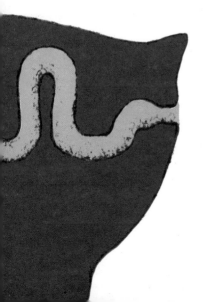

One sperm joins with one egg.

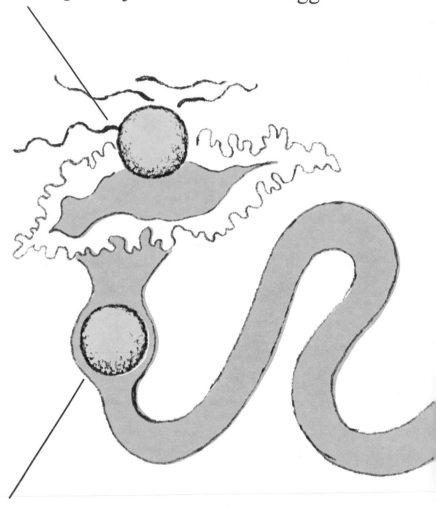

Then the egg goes down the tube.

On the way,

the white is added to the yolk.

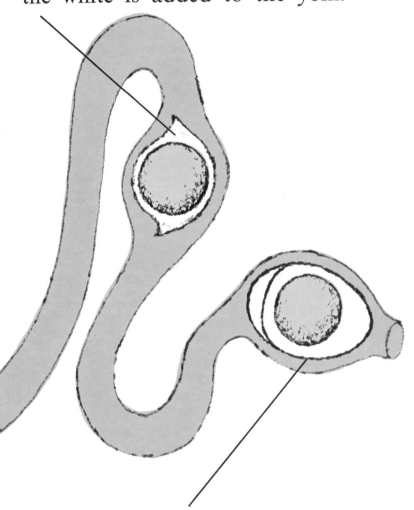

Then the shell is added.

Most of the eggs you buy

in the grocery store

have not been joined by sperm.

This is because the hens are kept
away from roosters.
That is why you cannot hatch a chick
from your breakfast egg.

Sometimes there are
little spots of blood
on the yolk of the egg.

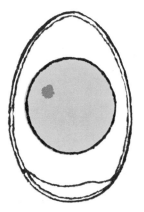

The blood spots get on the yolk

as it goes down the egg tube

before it is covered by the shell.

Blood spots do not mean the egg

is growing into a chicken.

This egg has been joined by a sperm.

It has just been laid by the hen.

The egg does not look like a chick.

But there is something in the egg

that can become a chick

in 21 days.

The inside of the egg looks like this.

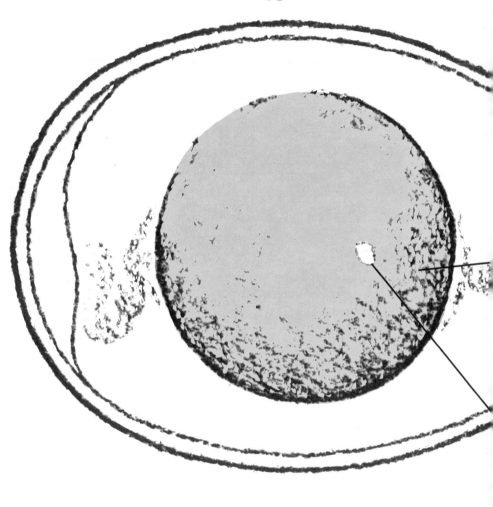

This is the white of the egg.

This is the yolk.

Have you looked at the white spot

on the yolk of an egg?

This white spot will grow

into a chick.

Heat makes the white spot

start to grow.

The mother hen

sits on her eggs.

She keeps them warm.

Then the eggs begin to change

into chicks.

Often the eggs are kept warm

in a box.

The box is heated by electricity.

It is called an incubator.

The egg has been kept warm

for 3 days.

See what has happened.

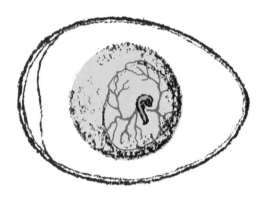

Look at the red lines

on the yolk.

They are little tubes

called blood vessels.

They carry blood to the growing chick.

The blood is full of food

from the yolk.

The tiny chick begins to grow.

It is called an embryo.

All animals are called embryos

when they first begin to grow.

Look at an embryo fish

and an embryo chick

and an embryo man.

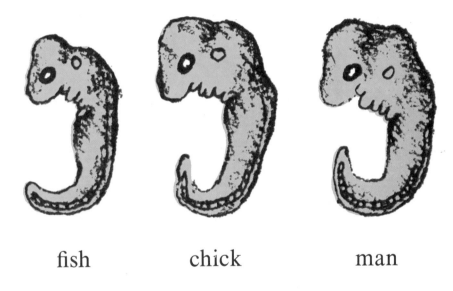

fish   chick   man

Do you see something strange?

The embryos look alike.

When the animals are bigger,

they will look very different.

But in the beginning,

the embryos look the same.

If you looked at

the 3-day-old embryo chick

through a magnifying glass,

this is what you would see.

the heart pumping blood ——

through the blood vessels

3 days

the eye

the head

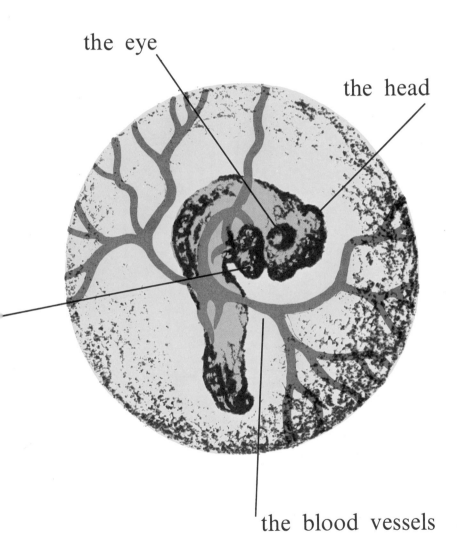

the blood vessels

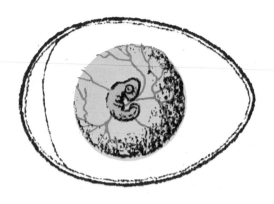

Now the egg has been kept warm

for 5 days.

The blood vessels

have grown longer and longer.

They cover almost the whole yolk.

How much bigger

the embryo has become!

The food from the yolk

is helping it grow.

5 days

Now, with a magnifying glass, you see

the ear

the heart

the eye

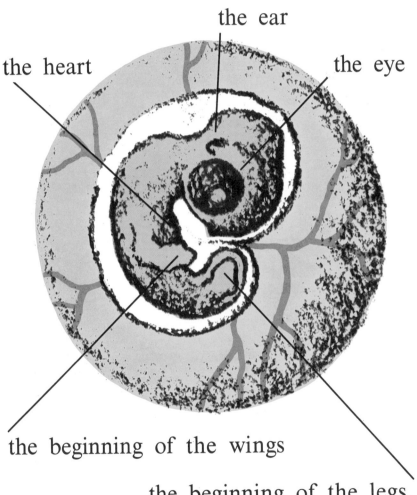

the beginning of the wings

the beginning of the legs.

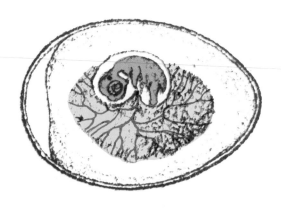

7 days old!

The embryo is only an inch long.

But all the parts of its body

have formed.

Its eyes and its head

are very big.

But the 7-day-old embryo

is beginning to look like a chick.

7 days

Do you see

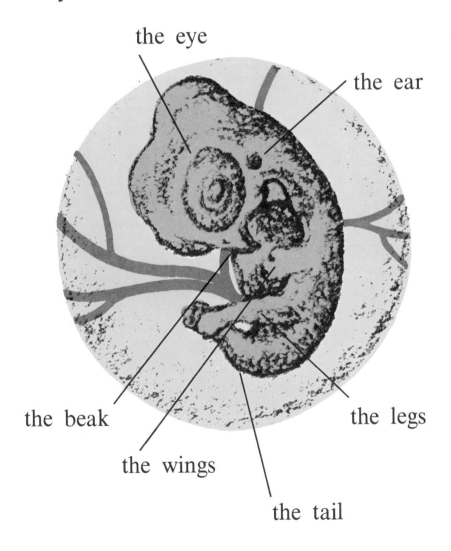

the eye

the ear

the beak

the wings

the tail

the legs

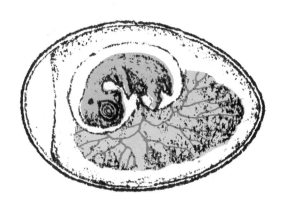

The 10-day-old embryo

is curled up on the yolk.

It looks like a little bird now,

but you can't see the feathers yet.

10 days

Look at the sac around the embryo.

It is like a plastic bag full of water.

It protects the embryo.

The embryo rocks in the sac.

When it is 13 days old,

the embryo looks like this.

Find the beak.

There is a special hard point

that sticks up at the tip.

It is called the egg tooth.

Later the egg tooth will help

to crack open the shell.

13 days

16 days old.

Only 5 more days to go

inside the egg.

Now the embryo really looks

like a chick.

Look at the feathers.

This is what is left of the yolk.

The white of the egg is almost gone.

It had lots of water in it

and a little food.

The growing embryo has used it up.

16 days

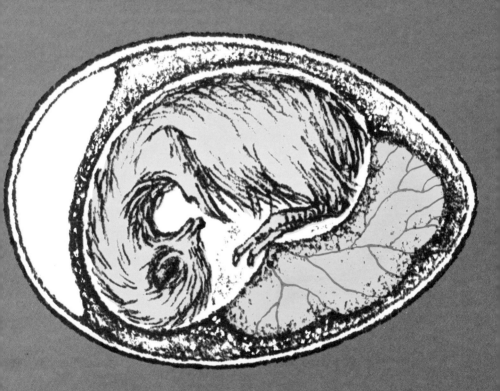

At 19 days

there is just a little yolk left.

See how much longer

the feathers are.

The feet are much bigger too.

The chick is almost ready

to come out of the egg.

19 days

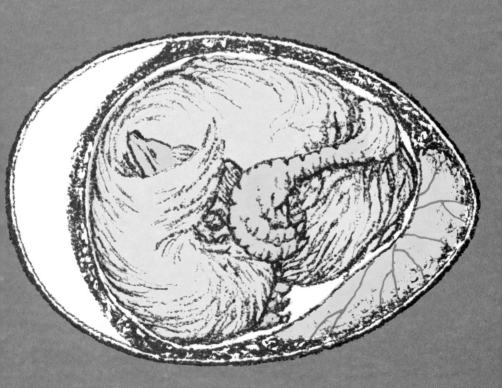

The 21 days inside the egg are over!

The chick pecks at the shell.

21 days

It pecks thousands of times.

At last the shell cracks.

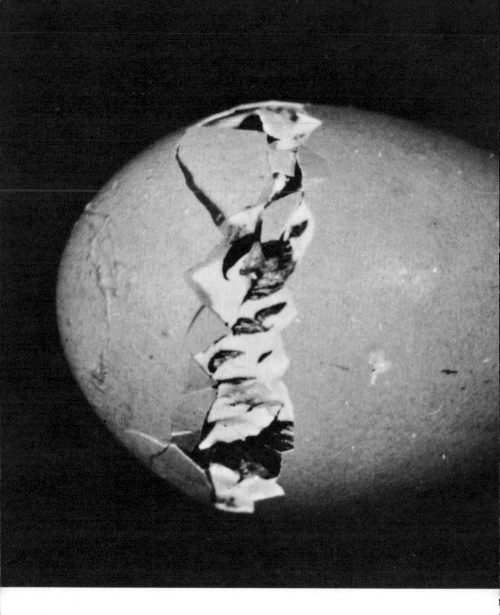

It is not easy for the chick
to get out.

It takes many hours to split

the shell all around.

51

Now the chick is almost out.

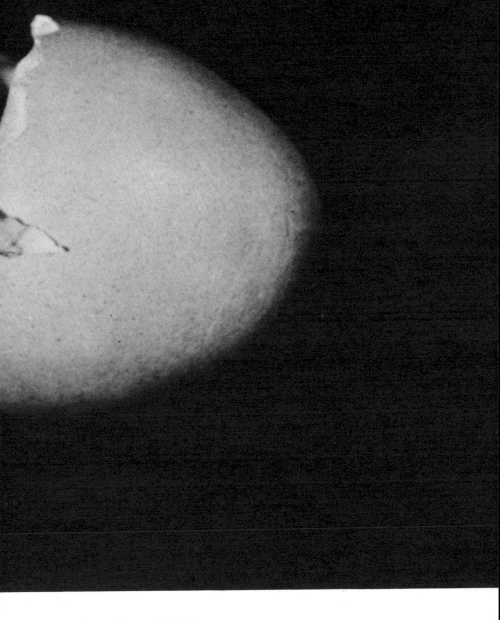

Slowly the chick

moves out of the shell.

The chick is still very weak.

Its legs are wobbly.

Its feathers are very wet.

In a few hours the feathers dry out.

Now the chick is soft and fluffy.

The hens lay more eggs
like these,

The chicks grow and grow and grow.

At last they become

hens and roosters like these.

The next day

the chick walks and runs about.

It picks up its food.

Most chicks are fed mashed seeds.

Mashed seeds look like

the cooked cereal

you eat for breakfast.